WORK

SUMMARY

FOR

Build the Life You Want

The Art and Science of Getting Happier

A Practical Guide To Arthur C. Brooks & Oprah Winfrey's Book

Jane press

This Book Belongs To

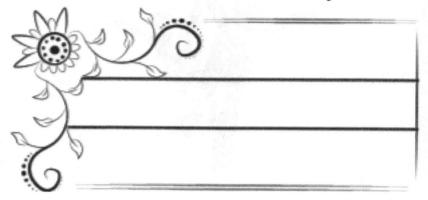

Disclaimer

This is a workbook for "Build the Life You Want: The Art and Science of Getting Happier
by Arthur C. Brooks , Oprah Winfrey
"

This Workbook information is not prepared to take the place of the original book. It serves as a
Tool to deepen the reader's comprehension.
Once again, the goal of this Workbook guide is to persuade the readers to purchase the original work in order to deepen their graps.

TABLE OF CONTENTS

HOW TO USE THIS WORKBOOK
SUMMARY
CHAPTER ONE: HAPPINESS IS NOT THE GOAL, AND UNHAPPINESS IS NOT THE ENEMY

key Lessons
Self-Reflection Questions
journals
Practical Action Exercises

CHAPTER TWO: THE POWER OF METACOGNITION

key Lessons
Self-Reflection Questions
journals
Practical Action Exercises

CHAPTER THREE: CHOOSE A BETTER EMOTION

key Lessons
Self-Reflection Questions
journals
Practical Action Exercises

CHAPTER FOUR: FOCUS LESS ON YOURSELF

key Lessons

Self-Reflection Questions

journals

Practical Action Exercises

CHAPTER FIVE: BUILD YOUR IMPERFECT FAMILY

key Lessons

Self-Reflection Questions

journals

Practical Action Exercises

CHAPTER SIX: FRIENDSHIP THAT IS DEEPLY REAL

key Lessons

Self-Reflection Questions

journals

Practical Action Exercises

CHAPTER SEVEN: WORK THAT IS LOVE MADE VISIBLE

key Lessons

Self-Reflection Questions

journals

Practical Action Exercises

CHAPTER EIGHT: FIND YOUR AMAZING GRACE

key Lessons
Self-Reflection Questions
journals
Practical Action Exercises

BONUS PACKAGE

- **30-Day happiness Living Challenge**
- **daily Happiness Assessment**
- **Goal Tracker**
- **Personal Affirmations**
- **Full Biography of Oprah Winfrey**

<u>HOW TO USE THIS WORKBOOK</u>

This workbook is intended to be your all-encompassing guide to altering your life and discovering ultimate happiness. This workbook will offer you with the skills and approaches to achieve personal growth, better relationships, or just greater joy in your daily life. We'll go through how to use this workbook successfully, how to explore its chapters, participate in self-reflection, actively apply the lessons, and how to use the accompanying journals to make the most of your road to a better life.:

1. Begin with the Summary:
Begin by reading the summary section to receive an overview of the workbook's core themes and aims. This will assist you in setting your goals and understanding what to anticipate from each part.

2. Explore the Chapters
Begin by becoming acquainted with the contents of the workbook. Each chapter has been meticulously developed to address various parts of your life that lead to happiness.

Take your time reading through the chapters, soaking in the information and thoughts.

4. Engage in Self-Reflections:
Throughout the workbook, you'll find self-reflection questions and prompts. Take the time to contemplate your thoughts, feelings, and experiences. Honest self-reflection is a powerful tool for personal growth and self-awareness.

5. Actively Apply the Lessons:
Happiness is not a passive pursuit. It necessitates action. Identify concrete activities you can take to incorporate the lessons into your everyday practice as you proceed through the workbook. Make a strategy and make a commitment to achieving positive changes in your life.

5. Actively Apply the Exercises:
Endeavour to actively participate in the given exercises, this will you help you get the most out of the workbook. The exercises are extracted from the information in the original book.

6. Use the Journals Provided:
Each chapter has its own journal space in this workbook. Use these notebooks to keep track of your ideas, goals, and progress. Writing down your experiences and thoughts may be an effective approach to keep track of your personal development path.

SUMMARY

The revolutionary book "Build the Life You Want: The Art and Science of Getting Happier" by Arthur C. Brooks and Oprah Winfrey explores the multidimensional road towards ultimate happiness. This outstanding cooperation between two renowned personalities digs into the subtle balance of art and science in producing a meaningful and joyous existence.

The book's central message is that happiness is not an abstract idea; rather, it is a measurable and attainable objective that anybody may pursue. Brooks and Winfrey take readers through the art of self-discovery, the science of happiness, and practical tactics for creating a life that resonates with their deepest wishes, drawing on their broad experience and knowledge.

The book begins with a fascinating examination of the art of happiness. Oprah Winfrey, recognized for her inspirational knowledge and ability to connect with people, presents personal tales and ideas that demonstrate the value of self-awareness, self-acceptance, and following one's passions. She highlights the need of developing one's inner world and discovering one's life's purpose.

Arthur C. Brooks, a renowned social scientist, adds the science of happiness to Winfrey's wisdom. He looks into the enormous study on positive psychology and well-being that has been undertaken.

Brooks discusses how appreciation, resilience, and healthy connections all play important parts in creating one's happiness and overall life satisfaction. He provides data-driven insights that help readers grasp the fundamental processes of happiness.

The writers smoothly integrate their ideas throughout the book, offering a comprehensive approach to happiness that is both accessible and practical. They inspire readers to go on a transformational journey by emphasizing the significance of having meaningful objectives and choosing values that resonate with one's actual self.

The power of choice is one of "Build the Life You Want"'s core themes. The writers underline that everyone, regardless of their life circumstances, have the ability to select their answers and build their own narratives. They inspire readers to abandon negative thought habits and embrace the possibility of development and transformation.

A substantial amount of the book is devoted to the significance of developing meaningful connections. Both writers emphasize the importance of genuine connections with people as a foundation for pleasure. They offer useful insights on successful communication, empathy, and vulnerability, all of which are necessary abilities for developing deeper, more rewarding relationships.

Brooks and Winfrey also discuss the significance of appreciation in the search of happiness. They explore how practicing thankfulness may change one's perspective, helping people to focus on the positive sides of life even when things are difficult. The book includes activities and strategies for infusing thankfulness into daily life.

Furthermore, the writers investigate the idea of resilience and how it leads to pleasure. They underline that while losses and hardship are unavoidable in life, people may learn to bounce back stronger and more resilient than before. Readers may manage life's problems more easily by adopting a growth mindset and establishing coping techniques.

"Build the Life You Want" emphasizes the significance of self-care and well-being. The writers emphasize the need of maintaining one's physical and mental health in order to achieve and maintain happiness. They offer advice and suggestions for living a balanced and healthy lifestyle that promotes general well-being.

The writers emphasize the need of self-reflection throughout the book. They urge readers to evaluate their beliefs, ambitions, and progress toward creating the life they want on a frequent basis. Self-reflection acts as a compass, guiding people to stay true to their actual selves and make necessary modifications along the path.

Arthur C. Brooks and Oprah Winfrey underscore the theme of giving back and finding meaning through service to others in the final chapters. They say that acts of compassion, giving, and contributing to the well-being of others are typically sources of real happiness. Individuals can enjoy a deeper and more lasting sort of happiness by cultivating a feeling of purpose beyond selfish fulfillment.

Arthur C. Brooks and Oprah Winfrey's "Build the Life You Want: The Art and Science of Getting Happier" is a comprehensive and inspiring analysis of the human search of happiness. The writers provide a complete guide to establishing a life that represents one's beliefs, interests, and goals through an engaging combination of personal experiences, scientific data, and practical guidance. This book inspires readers to go on a transforming path toward greater happiness, reminding us that the art and science of happiness are accessible to anybody prepared to take the first step.

as a way of life. Langer emphasizes that mindfulness is not a quick fix but a lifelong journey that can lead to profound changes in one's health and overall well-being. She leaves readers with the empowering message that they have the ability to shape their health and destiny through the power of their own minds.

In summary, "The Mindful Body: Thinking Our Way to Chronic Health" by Ellen J. Langer is a thought-provoking and inspiring exploration of the transformative potential of mindfulness in managing chronic health conditions. Langer's groundbreaking research, combined with her accessible writing style and practical guidance, makes this book a valuable resource for anyone seeking to improve their health and well-being. It challenges preconceived notions about chronic health issues, offering hope and empowerment to those willing to embark on a mindful journey towards better health. Ellen J. Langer's work serves as a beacon of light, illuminating the path to a healthier and more fulfilling life through the power of mindfulness.

GOAL TRACKER

MAIN GOAL

ACTION STEPS

1. _____
2. _____
3. _____

1. _____
2. _____
3. _____

GOAL 2

ACTION STEPS

1. _____
2. _____
3. _____
4. _____
5. _____
6. _____
7. _____

GOAL 3

ACTION STEPS

1. _____
2. _____
3. _____
4. _____
5. _____
6. _____
7. _____

GOAL 4

ACTION STEPS

1. _____
2. _____
3. _____
4. _____
5. _____
6. _____
7. _____

GOAL 5

ACTION STEPS

1. _____
2. _____
3. _____
4. _____
5. _____
6. _____
7. _____

30-Day Happiness Living Challenge

Day 01	Day 02	Day 03	Day 04	Day 05
5-minute to jot down what you're grateful for today	perform a random act of kindness to anybody	Use 10-minutes to perform deep mindful breathing	Disconnect yourself from social media for 1 day	Investigate Nature

Day 06	Day 07	Day 08	Day 09	Day 10
Show Your Appreciation to Someone	Experiment with Something New	Examine Your Achievements	Today, have a thoughtful lunch	Read a book, take a relaxing bath

Day 11	Day 12	Day 13	Day 14	Day 15
Contact a friend or family member you haven't spoken with in a long time	Today, be kind with yourself	sing or dance to your favorite music	A clean atmosphere can help you think more clearly.	Volunteer or Provide Assistance to Others

Day 16	Day 17	Day 18	Day 19	Day 20
Participate in an artistic hobby	Send a sincere note to your favorite person	Make any necessary changes.	Positive Affirmations for 3 days	Forgive someone who offended you in the past

Day 21	Day 22	Day 23	Day 24	Day 25
Visit a natural area that you enjoy	improve your digital life	Eat a Healthy Meal	Watch the sun rise or set	Show Your Love to someone

Day 26	Day 27	Day 28	Day 29	Day 30
Recognize your progress.	Write a letter of gratitude	Mindful nature walk or outdoor activity.	Deep Meditation.	Share your road to happiness with others

Name: _____   Date: _____

Daily happiness Assessment

Today is: _____

Current Level of Happiness:

Resilience

I'm grateful for...

_____
_____
_____
_____
_____
_____

Something new I learned today:

_____
_____
_____

CHAPTER ONE

Happiness Is Not the Goal , and Unhappiness is Not the Enemy

KEY LESSONS

- Pursuing pleasure as an end goal is frequently detrimental. Instead, it proposes that happiness be viewed as a result of living a satisfying and meaningful life.

- Unhappiness is a normal part of life, and it should not be regarded as something to be avoided at all costs. Unhappiness can provide inspiration for change and progress.

- The chapter dives into happiness research and how it is impacted by numerous elements such as genetics, circumstances, and deliberate behaviors. It emphasizes the concept that people have some influence over their happiness through their choices and activities.

- One of the most important lessons is the value of having a sense of purpose in life. People with a clear sense of purpose are happier and more resilient in the face of adversity.

- It is important individuals pursue significance and fulfillment in their life rather than pursuing transient moments of bliss. It implies that meaningful experiences and connections have a major impact on overall well-being.

How has my major objective of happiness influenced my life decisions and priorities thus far?

_____

_____

_____

_____

_____

Can I think of any times when being unhappy or uncomfortable resulted in personal growth or beneficial improvements in my life?

_____

_____

_____

_____

_____

What are some strategies for changing my mindset such that I perceive misery as a possible spark for self-improvement and resilience?

_____

_____

_____

_____

Is it possible that I have been too concerned with avoiding unpleasant feelings, and if so, how has this damaged my general well-being?

_____

_____

_____

_____

What role does a sense of purpose and meaning play in my life, and how can I consciously incorporate it to attain long-term fulfillment?

_____

_____

_____

_____

How do I find a balance between seeking happiness and appreciating the importance of experiencing the entire range of human emotions and experiences?

_____

_____

_____

_____

Workbook Exercise

Instructions:

- Make a scale of 1 to 10, with 1 representing "Utterly Unhappy" and 10 representing "Euphorically Happy."

- Consider your regular emotional state on a typical day. Mark the point on the scale where you feel your average emotional state falls.

- Consider a recent occurrence or scenario that made you unpleasant or uneasy. Make a note of where this particular feeling stands on the scale.

- Consider a recent occurrence or scenario that has brought you joy or happiness. Make a note of where this particular feeling stands on the scale.

- Consider the variations in your typical emotional state, the sadness point, and the happy point on the scale.

JOURNAL

PERSONAL NOTES

"I am the architect of my life, and I have the power to create the happiness I desire."

Name: _____ Date: _____

Daily happiness Assessment

Today is:

Current Level of Happiness:

Resilience

I'm grateful for...

_____

_____

_____

_____

_____

_____

Something new I learned today:

_____

_____

_____

CHAPTER TWO

The Power of Metacognition

KEY LESSONS

- Metacognition is the ability to think about and regulate one's own thoughts. It highlights the importance of understanding and regulating our ideas and thinking patterns for personal progress and pleasure.

- the importance of becoming aware of our automatic thought processes and how they might effect our emotions and behavior. It enables readers to recognize negative thought patterns that may be impeding their progress.

- It addresses ways for replacing negative thought patterns with more positive and helpful ones. This involves cognitive reframing and mindfulness practices.

- The importance of self-compassion in metacognition is emphasized in this chapter. It implies that being kind and understanding to oneself, particularly during difficult circumstances, may lead to greater satisfaction and personal progress.

- Developing metacognitive abilities necessitates effort and perseverance. It invites readers to commit to constant self-reflection and mindfulness in order to properly harness the potential of metacognition.

How frequently do I pause to consider my own
thinking patterns and how they influence my
emotions and actions?

_____

_____

_____

_____

Can I recognize repeating negative thinking
patterns that may be impeding my personal
progress and happiness?

_____

_____

_____

_____

_____

How successful were the tactics I employed in the past to modify negative thinking patterns

_____

_____

_____

_____

Do I give myself compassion and understanding when I detect detrimental thinking patterns, or am I being too harsh on myself?

_____

_____

_____

_____

_____

What steps can I take to incorporate mindfulness
and self-awareness into my everyday routine to
improve my metacognitive abilities?

_____

_____

_____

_____

What concrete measures can I take to practice
and strengthen my metacognitive abilities in
order to increase my general well-being?

_____

_____

_____

_____

Workbook Exercise

Instructions:

- Make a special time for self-reflection.

- Keep a record of your thoughts and emotions for one week. Keep a notebook and write down any powerful emotions or repeated thoughts you have.

- Review your diary entries at the end of the week.

- Identify any recurring thinking patterns or topics in your diary. Self-criticism, concern about the future, or brooding on past mistakes are examples.

- List at least three thinking patterns you've identified and offer a brief explanation of each in the area below.

JOURNAL

PERSONAL NOTES

"I have embraced the art of gratitude, finding joy in life's simple moments."

Name: _____   Date: _____

Daily happiness Assessment

Today is:

Current Level of Happiness:

Resilience	I'm grateful for...
	_____
	_____
	_____
	_____
	_____
	_____
	_____

Something new I learned today:

_____
_____
_____

CHAPTER THREE

<u>Choose a Better Emotion</u>

KEY LESSONS

- We can see in this chapter that we have the ability to pick our feelings. It underlines the fact that we have the ability to actively choose how we want to feel in response to various events and obstacles in our life.

- The notion of emotional reframing is altering how we perceive and respond to unfavorable feelings. We may transform our emotions into chances for personal growth and resilience by reframing them.

- Emotional Agility: The chapter presents the concept of emotional agility, which is the capacity to efficiently navigate and adapt to various emotions. It implies that emotional agility is an important talent for living a better and more satisfying life.

-

- This chapter looks at how to cultivate healthy emotional habits including appreciation, compassion, and mindfulness. These practices can assist us in shifting our emotional state toward more pleasant and gratifying emotions.

- The ripple effect of emotions and how our emotional choices affect not just our personal well-being but also the well-being of people around us. Choosing more happy emotions can result in more good encounters and relationships.

How frequently do I deliberately choose my emotions in response to difficult events or unfavorable experiences?

_____

_____

_____

_____

Is there a recent instance in which I effectively reframed a bad mood into a more positive one? What was the end result?

_____

_____

_____

_____

_____

Do I exercise emotional agility, that is, am I versatile and resilient while dealing with various emotions in my life?

_____

_____

_____

_____

What are my present emotional habits, and how do they affect my general well-being and interactions with others?

_____

_____

_____

_____

_____

Have I examined how my emotions affect people around me? How can I make more deliberate decisions to foster a pleasant emotional climate in my relationships and interactions?

_____

_____

_____

_____

_____

What tactics or approaches can I use in my everyday life to constantly pick healthier feelings and promote emotional well-being?

_____

_____

_____

_____

_____

Workbook Exercise

Instructions:

- Consider a recent scenario or encounter that elicited a negative emotional response in you. It might be disappointment, rage, grief, or any other unpleasant feeling.

- Fill in the blanks with a brief summary of the scenario.

JOURNAL

PERSONAL NOTES

_____

_____

_____

_____

_____

_____

_____

_____

_____

_____

_____

_____

_____

_____

_____

_____

_____

_____

"*I am open to the science of happiness and am constantly learning and growing.*"

Name: _____ Date: _____

Daily happiness Assessment

Today is:

Current Level of Happiness:

Resilience

I'm grateful for...

_____
_____
_____
_____
_____
_____
_____

Something new I learned today:

_____
_____
_____

KEY LESSONS

- The chapter delves into the paradox of excessive self-focus and self-absorption leading to sadness and solitude. It demonstrates how transferring one's attention away from oneself may lead to greater fulfillment.

- It highlights the value of interacting with people and developing meaningful connections. The chapter addresses the beneficial effects of social ties on happiness and well-being.

- The chapter looks on the concept of doing acts of kindness for others in order to increase one's own happiness. It delves into the notion of "helper's high" and how helping others may provide a feeling of purpose and fulfillment.

- It goes through the practice of thankfulness and how concentrating on the positive things of life may help you be happier. The value of gratitude exercises and recognising and appreciating the positive in life are discussed.

- According to the chapter, transcending the ego and discovering a sense of purpose beyond personal needs can lead to a more meaningful and rewarding existence. It inspires readers to strive for a higher purpose or to contribute to a cause larger than themselves.

How frequently do I become obsessed with my own wants, desires, and concerns, and how does this affect my overall happiness?

_____

_____

_____

_____

Can I think of times in my life when interacting with others and developing meaningful connections provided me joy and fulfillment?

_____

_____

_____

_____

_____

What specific acts of kindness or charity have I
lately committed, and how did they make me
feel?

_____

_____

_____

_____

_____

Do I express thankfulness on a daily basis, and if
so, how does it affect my outlook on life and
general feeling of well-being?

_____

_____

_____

_____

_____

Have I ever had a feeling of purpose or pleasure from contributing to a cause or activity that is larger than my own personal interests and desires?

_____

_____

_____

_____

_____

What measures can I take in my everyday life to change my emphasis away from myself and toward more meaningful connections, acts of kindness, appreciation, and a feeling of purpose?

_____

_____

_____

_____

_____

Workbook Exercise

Instructions:

- For the following week, set aside a few minutes each day to perform this practice.

- Make a daily post in a diary or on paper labeled "Gratitude Journal."

- Write down three things you are grateful for every day. These might be little or major events in your life.

- After you've written down your daily gratitudes, take a minute to consider how these objects or experiences are related to people or circumstances outside of yourself.

- Write a summary of your reflections and how concentrating on thankfulness has helped you shift your emphasis away from yourself and toward appreciation for others and the environment around you in the area below.

JOURNAL

_____

PERSONAL NOTES

_____

_____

_____

_____

_____

_____

_____

_____

_____

_____

_____

_____

_____

_____

_____

_____

_____

"*I choose to focus on what truly matters, nurturing meaningful connections.*"

Name: _____   Date: _____

Daily happiness Assessment

Today is: _____

Current Level of Happiness:

Resilience

I'm grateful for...

_____
_____
_____
_____
_____
_____

Something new I learned today:

_____
_____
_____

CHAPTER FIVE

Build Your Imperfect Family

KEY LESSONS

- The chapter delves into the premise that families, like all human interactions, are flawed. It emphasizes how unreasonable aspirations of perfection can lead to family disappointment and misery.

- It highlights the value of unconditional love within families, where members embrace each other's defects and shortcomings. Despite familial differences, this lesson encourages readers to foster love and understanding.

- The importance of successful communication and emotional connection within families is discussed in this chapter. It emphasizes the need of open and honest interactions in fostering trust and strengthening familial relationships.

- It looks at forgiveness and the ability to let go of grudges or previous injuries within the family. Forgiveness is provided as a means of achieving healing and peace.

- The chapter urges readers to devote time and effort in developing and fostering strong family ties. It underlines the importance of these relationships in overall happiness and well-being.

How do my family's demands of perfection contribute to emotions of disappointment or irritation, and how can I change these expectations to foster happiness and harmony?

_____

_____

_____

_____

_____

What are some particular situations in my family when I have practiced unconditional love and acceptance, and how have these experiences impacted our relationships?

_____

_____

_____

_____

_____

Do I actively participate in open and honest conversation with my family members, or is there anything I can do better to deepen our bonds?

_____

_____

_____

_____

Is there anything unresolved in my family that I can work on forgiving and letting go of? How can I use this forgiveness to help myself and my family?

_____

_____

_____

_____

_____

What actions can I take to actively establish and cultivate strong connections within my family, creating an atmosphere of love, trust, and suppor

_____

_____

_____

_____

_____

In what ways can I help to make my family a place where flaws are celebrated and love and understanding reign supreme?

_____

_____

_____

_____

_____

Workbook Exercise

Instructions:

- Choose a family member with whom you have an unsolved disagreement. This might be a parent, sibling, relative, or any other member of your family.

- Consider the disagreement or issue and how it has impacted you and your connection with that family member.

- Write a letter of apology to this family member. The letter states:
  1. Describe your emotions and ideas on the disagreement or topic.
  2. Declare that you forgive them for any wrongdoing and that you are ready to let go of any grudge or bad emotions.
  3. Express your wish to repair or enhance your connection with them, stressing your love and gratitude.

- Read the forgiveness letter aloud to yourself when you've finished it. This may be an effective technique to communicate your intentions and feelings.

- Consider sharing the letter with the family member if you feel comfortable and believe it is appropriate. It's OK, though, if you choose to keep it private for your own personal development.

JOURNAL

PERSONAL NOTES

"I am resilient in the face of challenges, knowing that they are opportunities for growth."

Name: _____   Date: _____

Daily happiness Assessment

Today is:
_____

Current Level of Happiness:

Resilience

I'm grateful for...
_____
_____
_____
_____
_____
_____

Something new I learned today:
_____
_____
_____

CHAPTER SIX

KEY LESSONS

- The chapter stresses the value of genuine, meaningful friendships in our life. It implies that true connections with people might have a substantial impact on our pleasure and general well-being.

- It explores the notion of shared vulnerability within friendships, where people feel secure and comfortable sharing their genuine selves, including worries and vulnerabilities, with one another.

- The chapter emphasizes the notion that the quality of friendships is more important than the quantity. Having a small circle of genuine and true connections might be more gratifying than a big number of acquaintances.

- It urges readers to put time and effort into cultivating and keeping meaningful connections. To thrive, these interactions demand attention, care, and reciprocity.

- The chapter emphasizes the mutual support and progress that may happen in genuine friendships. It implies that these interactions, via shared experiences and understanding, create a framework for personal development and enjoyment.

What features and attributes do I appreciate the most
in my closest friendships, and how do these qualities
contribute to the depth of these relationships?

_____

_____

_____

_____

Has my willingness to be vulnerable and speak
up about my genuine self with my closest
friends affected the validity of our friendships?

_____

_____

_____

_____

Do I value quality above number in my friendships, and how may concentrating on deeper relationships improve my general well-being?

_____

_____

_____

_____

_____

How much time and effort do I put into cultivating and preserving my close connections, and how has this commitment benefited their strength?

_____

_____

_____

_____

_____

Can I think of times when my genuine friendships gave mutual support and opportunity for personal growth, and how these events enhanced my life?

_____

_____

_____

_____

What measures can I take to build and enhance my existing friendships or seek out new connections that share the characteristics of profoundly genuine friendships

_____

_____

_____

_____

_____

Workbook Exercise

Instructions:

- Choose a close friend who has had a significant influence on your life and whom you genuinely admire.

- Consider the characteristics and experiences that make this friendship unique and real.

- Write a genuine thank you note to your buddy.

- After you've finished drafting the letter, read it aloud to yourself. Allow yourself to fully accept sentiments of thankfulness and appreciation.

- Consider sharing the letter with your buddy as a token of thanks if you feel comfortable doing so. It is, however, acceptable to keep it private if it is your desire.

-

JOURNAL

PERSONAL NOTES

"I practice self-compassion and forgiveness, releasing the weight of my past mistakes."

Name: _____   Date: _____

Daily happiness Assessment

Today is:

Current Level of Happiness:

Resilience

I'm grateful for...

_____

_____

_____

_____

_____

_____

_____

Something new I learned today:

_____

_____

_____

CHAPTER SEVEN

<u>Work that Is Love Made Visible</u>

KEY LESSONS

- The chapter emphasizes the concept that work may give pleasure and fulfillment if it corresponds with one's beliefs and provides a feeling of purpose. Meaningful employment is depicted as an important factor to overall happiness.

- It underlines the significance of pursuing employment that is in line with one's interests and calling. According to the chapter, aligning one's work with one's own beliefs and interests might result in a more full and gratifying professional life.

- When employment incorporates service and giving to others, it becomes an expression of love. It emphasizes the satisfaction that comes from having a positive effect on others via one's work.

- It highlights the need of balancing professional achievement with personal well-being. According to the chapter, focusing entirely on external successes might sometimes come at the price of happiness.

- Continuous personal and professional development and learning are vital for long-term career happiness. It emphasizes the need of adaptation and a development attitude.

Is my present job bringing me joy and fulfillment, and does it connect with my own beliefs and passions?

_____

_____

_____

_____

_____

What components of my work or profession are meaningful to me and contribute to my general well-being?

_____

_____

_____

_____

_____

In what ways does my career allow me to assist others and have a good influence on their lives, and how does this element of my profession make me happy?

_____

_____

_____

_____

_____

Is it possible for me to strike a good balance between achieving professional success and preserving my personal well-being and happiness?

_____

_____

_____

_____

_____

How do I accept chances for career growth and learning, and how have these experiences affected my feeling of fulfillment?

_____

_____

_____

_____

Can I imagine improvements or adjustments to my work that would put it more in line with the notion of "work that is love made visible," and if so, what actions can I take to get there?

_____

_____

_____

_____

_____

Workbook Exercise

Instructions:

- Find a calm, meditative area where you may concentrate on your profession and job.

- Take a few moments to consider what the phrase "work that is love made visible" means to you. What does your ideal work environment look like?

- Consider your desired career or work. What type of career would actually match your interests, values, and feeling of purpose? What effect would it have on others' well-being and enjoyment, as well as your own?

- Create a personal work vision statement outlining your dream profession or position. This should be a brief, forceful statement expressing your desire to do something that is a representation of love and purpose.

- Take some time to think about your vision statement once you've written it. What effect does it have on you? How does that relate to your present situation at work? Is there anything particular you can think of to get closer to this ideal?

JOURNAL

PERSONAL NOTES

"I am committed to aligning my work with my passions and purpose, as well as finding fulfillment in my career."

Name: _____   Date: _____

Daily happiness Assessment

Today is: _____

Current Level of Happiness:

Resilience

I'm grateful for...

_____
_____
_____
_____
_____
_____
_____

Something new I learned today:

_____
_____
_____

CHAPTER EIGHT

Find Your Amazing Grace

KEY LESSONS

- The topic of forgiveness and its transformational influence on one's well-being is explored in this chapter. It highlights the need of forgiving others as well as oneself in order to achieve better pleasure and inner peace.

- It explains the harmful consequences of harboring hatred and grudges. According to the chapter, releasing these negative feelings via forgiveness is critical for personal growth and happiness.

- The chapter emphasizes the value of self-compassion and self-forgiveness. It urges readers to be kind and accepting of themselves, acknowledging that everyone makes errors.

- It dives into gratitude's healing power and the role it plays in discovering one's magnificent grace. The exercises and practices of gratitude are provided as strategies for fostering inner serenity.

- the importance of connecting with those who have gone through forgiveness and transformation. It tells the experiences of people who have discovered their tremendous grace through forgiveness and perseverance.

Have I had experiences where forgiveness,
whether towards others or myself, aided my
own growth and happiness?

_____

_____

_____

_____

Are there any residual grudges or resentments
in my life that I may benefit from forgiving and
letting go of?

_____

_____

_____

_____

_____

When I make errors or confront problems in my life, how do I practice self-compassion and self-forgiveness?

_____

_____

_____

_____

_____

Do I practice thankfulness on a regular basis, and how does it affect my sense of inner peace and well-being?

_____

_____

_____

_____

_____

Can I think of times in my life when I met someone who had achieved incredible grace through forgiveness and resilience? What effect did these relationships have on me?

_____

_____

_____

_____

_____

What actions can I do to actively develop forgiveness, appreciation, and self-compassion in my life, therefore promoting my own journey toward discovering my great grace?

_____

_____

_____

_____

_____

Workbook Exercise

Instructions:

- Find a quiet, comfortable spot to think about self-forgiveness.

- Consider a specific error or regret from your past that still bothers you. It might be a mistake you committed or a scenario in which you believe you failed yourself.

- Write a letter of forgiveness to yourself, addressing this previous wrong or regret.

- After you've finished drafting the forgiveness letter, read it aloud to yourself. Allow yourself to be moved by the words of forgiveness and self-compassion.

- Consider how this activity makes you feel. Has it assisted you in discovering a sense of incredible grace within yourself? How may releasing this weight improve your general well-being?

JOURNAL

PERSONAL NOTES

"I believe in my ability to find my own amazing grace through forgiveness, resilience, and gratitude."

BIOGRAPHY OF OPRAH WINFREY

Oprah Winfrey was a young girl in the 1950s who loved to tell stories and lived on her grandparents' farm outside Kosciusko, Mississippi. She named her farm animals and told them stories, some of which were made up and others came from the Bible. Her grandmother Hattie Mae Lee used the Bible to teach her to read at an early age, and she was smart and memorized Bible verses easily. She began reciting Bible verses at her church on Easter Sunday in 1957, and as she got older, she spoke at other churches and recited longer passages from the Bible.

Oprah was born on January 29, 1954, in Kosciusko, Mississippi, to Vernita Lee and Vernon Winfrey, who was in the US Army. When her mother moved to Milwaukee for the summer, she was left alone at home, with her brother and sister, Patricia, and Jeffrey sharing one bedroom. Her father, Vernon Winfrey, was in the US Army and did not know he would be a father when he returned to the army base in Alabama.

In 1963, Oprah returned to Milwaukee for the summer, but her mother did not want her to leave. She stayed in Milwaukee, and she began the new school year in Milwaukee. At home, she was lonely, and she spent much of her time looking after her younger siblings. She also read and watched television, enjoying shows about happy families and funny shows like I Love Lucy.

When Oprah was nine, an older cousin hurt her in her most private places, and over the next five years, the abuse happened with relatives and a friend of the family. Oprah never told anyone about her experiences, believing that no one would believe her. She never told anyone, and today she encourages people to tell someone if they don't believe you.

One of Oprah's middle-school teachers noticed that Oprah didn't act like the other students and helped her get into Upward Bound, a program that taught low-income students the skills they needed to attend college. Through Upward Bound, Oprah began classes at Nicolet High School, which was about twenty miles from her home.

The students at Nicolet were friendly to Oprah, but she began getting into trouble herself. One time, she even ran away from home. Her mother asked Vernon Winfrey to come and bring her back, but they soon discovered that fourteen-year-old Oprah was pregnant. She gave birth to a baby boy who died too early and later died. Oprah was sad but determined to try to change her life for the better.

Vernon, Oprah's father, desired that she modify her life and put a stop to her wild ways. He had her wash off her heavy makeup and short, tight skirts, set a bedtime for her, and expected her to study hard in school. Oprah began tenth grade at East High School in Nashville in September 1968, becoming one of the school's first black pupils. She was given extra tasks, such as learning twenty new vocabulary words each week and reading five novels and writing reports on them every two weeks.

Oprah was an excellent student in high school and joined a public speaking group. She was chosen, along with another student, to represent Tennessee at the White House Conference on Youth in Colorado in 1971.

When Oprah returned home, John Heidelberg of Nashville's WVOL radio station interviewed her and asked if she would represent the station in the Miss Fire Prevention beauty competition. Oprah won the contest and became Nashville's first African American Miss Fire Prevention.

John Heidelberg aired the recording for the station management, who gave her a position at WVOL during her tenure there. She listened to the news on the radio after school and on weekends when she was seventeen years old. In June 1971, she graduated from high school and enrolled at Tennessee State University, paying for her tuition using a scholarship she received for a speech she made in a competition. Oprah studied speech and theatre in college, aspiring to be an actor. She also competed in beauty pageants, winning the titles of Miss Black Nashville and Miss Black Tennessee.

A local TV station asked Oprah to audition for the position of co-anchor (news presenter) of the evening news in 1973.

She claimed to be Barbara Walters for the audition, which went well, and she went on to become Nashville's first black television news anchor and female newscaster. She was the city's youngest newscaster at the age of nineteen.

Oprah did not graduate with the rest of her college classmates in 1975, and she dropped out after only one class. In 1976, she received an even greater offer from WJZ-TV in Baltimore, Maryland, which marked a significant advancement in her career. Despite her stern father's severe regulations, Oprah took the job and relocated to Maryland.

Oprah has always valued her reading. She wanted to share her passion for books with others, so she founded Oprah's Book Club in 1996. Oprah chose a book to discuss on her talk program. She had to wait a month for anyone to read it. Then the entire show would be devoted to discussing the book. People who have read the book were in Oprah's audience. Occasionally, the author would appear as a guest on the show.

Every book Oprah chose for her book club sold really well.

The majority of the novels she chose sold more than a million copies. Oprah was overjoyed with the messages she received from her fans. Some people claimed they hadn't read a book in years. They were reading again, and they were enjoying it.

Oprah also encouraged her audience to help others. She has donated millions of dollars to libraries, colleges, and children's activities. She gave college scholarships to deserving youngsters. She also enabled low-income children to attend prep schools to better prepare them for college, as Upward Bound had done for her. Oprah had the means to make enormous charitable contributions, but she realized that even tiny contributions could make a difference. In 1998, she launched Oprah's Angel Network, inviting her admirers to donate their spare coins. The funds were deposited in what became known as "the World's Largest Piggy Bank." In its first year, the Angel Network raised more than $3.5 million! That initiative provided scholarships to 150 young individuals over the next three years. Each was valued at $25,000. Angel Network funds have also been donated to Habitat for Humanity.

Volunteers assist in the construction of homes for persons who cannot afford them through this initiative. The Angel Network has helped to build women's shelters, juvenile shelters, and schools in many nations throughout the world.

People believed Oprah because she was so kind. They paid close attention to what she had to say. Oprah hosted a broadcast in 1996 that featured a topic about risky foods. One of the guests on the broadcast discussed mad cow disease and how it may spread to people who ate meat from afflicted animals.

Oprah stated on the episode, "It has just stopped me cold from eating another burger." Beef sales dropped after the episode, and cattle farmers in Texas blamed Oprah. The Texas Beef Group sued her in 1997, seeking more than $10 million in damages. It would have been simple for Oprah to just pay them, but she chose not to. She felt she had a right to conduct shows about critical issues like mad cow disease.

She was prepared to go to court to fight for that right. The trial began in Amarillo, Texas, in January 1998. It was six weeks long.

Oprah continued to host her show throughout this period. Her days were spent in court. She taped her program in the evenings at the Amarillo Little Theatre after a meal break. On February 26, the court concluded that Oprah was not to blame for the drop in beef sales. Oprah rejoiced outside the courthouse. "Free speech not only lives, it rocks!" she said, pumping her hands in the air.

Oprah has won seven Daytime Emmy Awards for outstanding talk-show host by 1998. She was awarded an Emmy for Lifetime Achievement the same year. Barbara Walters gave the prize to Oprah, thanking her for her charitable work. "The only thing greater than Oprah's accomplishments is the size of her heart," Barbara said.

Oprah was busy filming movies in addition to hosting her talk show. She had a deal with the ABC television network to make six made-for-television movies. Oprah also produced a film based on a book she adored. Toni Morrison's award-winning novel Beloved tells the narrative of a former slave who is plagued by her past.

Oprah played the part of Sethe, a former slave, in the film. In October 1998, Beloved was released in cinemas. The performance, particularly Oprah's, was praised by film reviewers. They also complained that the three-hour film was too lengthy and that the plot was confused. Ticket sales were disappointing. Oprah thought it was a significant story. She was disappointed that no one came to see it. One of Oprah's biggest disappointments was the failure of Beloved. But, as usual, she did not give up. She progressed to new and larger tasks.

Oprah joined the publishing sector in 2000, with O, the Oprah Magazine. It built on the themes presented on Oprah's show and brought them to a wider audience. Women who couldn't get enough of Oprah now had a magazine to look forward to. Oprah's mission of helping others live their greatest lives was reaching more people than ever before.

A new magazine may take several years to find readers. O, the Oprah Magazine was an instant hit. There were 1.9 million members within a few months. Gayle King, Oprah's best friend, was chosen editor-at-large for the magazine.

Gayle reports to Oprah, who has the final call on which pieces to feature each month. Every issue features Oprah on the cover. Oprah had gone a long way from being a barefoot young girl on a Mississippi plantation.

She had, nevertheless, never lost her affection for the land. She purchased a 42-acre estate in Montecito, California, in 2001. She could see the ocean from her house. She built an oak tree forest, a fountain, and a big garden. She purchased land in Hawaii in 2002. She also produces fruits and veggies there. Harvest days, according to Oprah, are some of her happiest times. She still enjoys cultivating the food she consumes.

Oprah also kept looking for ways to help people. In 2002, she flew to South Africa to provide toys, books, school materials, and clothing to 50,000 youngsters. It was the first time most of the youngsters had ever gotten a gift. Oprah revealed her intention to construct the Oprah Winfrey Leadership Academy for Girls during her tour. The residential school would be constructed in a community approximately an hour's drive from Johannesburg.

Oprah was engaged in every aspect of the planning, including the design of the dorm rooms. She also assisted with the selection of pupils who would live and study at the institution. They were picked for their need, talent, and leadership abilities. Oprah sought pupils who would utilize their education to improve South Africa. The school opened in 2007 after five years of hard labor.

Oprah considers the young ladies at the school to be family. She had frequently considered having children, but there never seemed to be a right moment. Oprah said in 2009 that The Oprah Winfrey Show will terminate after the 2010-2011 season. The choice to end the program was painful, but Oprah thought it was the perfect moment. "This show has been my life," she remarked, adding, "and I love it enough to know when it's time to say goodbye." After twenty-five seasons, the last episode aired on May 25, 2011. But Oprah has no intention of slowing down. She had previously formed a partnership with Discovery Communications to launch OWN (the Oprah Winfrey Network). On January 1, 2011, it began airing.

Oprah made an investment in Weight Watchers International, Inc. in 2015. When she was really busy or worried, she occasionally neglected to consume nutritious meals and exercise. Then she put on weight. She was attempting to lose weight once more, so she attempted the Weight Watchers program. She concluded the training worked and the firm was a worthwhile investment after dropping fourteen pounds. She purchased a 10% stake in the firm.

Oprah had a very busy year in 2017. Her cookbook, Food, Health, and Happiness, was launched in January. The dishes were created in collaboration with some of her favorite chefs. She also shared family photographs and memories from her life.

Oprah has collaborated with a team of chefs to develop her own line of packaged meals called O, That's Good!, which includes soups and side dishes. Ten percent of O, That's Good! revenues are donated to the organizations Rise Against Hunger and Feeding America. She began working as a special correspondent on the evening news show 60 Minutes that fall.

Oprah is still producing and acting in films, such as The Immortal Life of Henrietta Lacks. She came to New Zealand to shoot her role as Mrs. Which, a wise guide, in A Wrinkle in Time, based on Madeleine L'Engle's popular novel.

Oprah was recognized during the Golden Globes award ceremony in 2018 with the Cecil B. DeMille Award. It is named after the legendary director and is presented each year to someone who has made "outstanding contributions to the world of entertainment." Oprah was the first African American woman to be honored in this way. Most people remember Oprah's strong acceptance speech from that night. She earned multiple standing ovations as she spoke about the need of speaking up when those in authority are wronging you. "Speaking your truth is the most powerful tool we all have," she asserted.

The next morning, the Internet was ablaze with headlines like "Oprah for President!" Oprah may not be fully qualified to be president, but many people hoped she would run. It demonstrated how much people believe in and trust Oprah.

Oprah used to tell stories to the pigs and poultry on her grandparents' farm when she was a child. Her voice is now heard all over the world. She is a Hollywood titan who has done it all: she has been the star of her own television program, an actor, and a film producer. She also writes, publishes magazines, and has her own television network. She is also referred to as the "Master of Media." Her hard work has made her one of the world's wealthiest and most influential women. But Oprah is most recognized for her ongoing efforts to assist and inspire people. Oprah remains a trusted and loyal friend to people who have watched her television show, read her magazine, and heeded her counsel.